כִּי מִצִּיּוֹן

Which objects, or things that you do, link you to your past *and* to your future? If your mom gives you her wedding dress to wear when you get married, and you pass that dress on to your own daughter, you have created a chain linking your past and your future together. If your dad gives you his vintage baseball cards, and you someday give them to your own son or daughter, you also create such a chain. In the same way, the Torah links us to our ancestors and to our descendants. From generation to generation, the teachings of the Torah are passed down as we read it each week, creating an unending chain of knowledge and tradition, and building our heritage.

כִּי מִצִּיּוֹן, the prayer that we say as we remove the Torah from the Ark, connects us to our ancient past and to our future. It expresses our hope and our belief that both the Torah and the land of Israel will continue to be our source of spiritual strength for generations to come.

We stand as the Ark is opened.

Practice reading כִּי מִצִּיּוֹן **aloud.**

1. כִּי מִצִּיּוֹן תֵּצֵא תוֹרָה, וּדְבַר־יְיָ מִירוּשָׁלָיִם.
2. בָּרוּךְ שֶׁנָּתַן תּוֹרָה לְעַמּוֹ יִשְׂרָאֵל בִּקְדֻשָּׁתוֹ.

For out of Zion shall go forth Torah, and the word of God from Jerusalem.
Praised is the One, who in holiness gave the Torah to God's people Israel.

מִצִּיּוֹן

from Zion

תּוֹרָה

Torah, teaching

וּדְבַר

and the word of

מִירוּשָׁלָיִם

from Jerusalem

שֶׁנָּתַן

who gave

לְעַמּוֹ

to God's people

בִּקְדֻשָּׁתוֹ

in God's holiness

MATCH GAME

Connect each Hebrew word to its English meaning.

to God's people   תּוֹרָה

from Zion   וּדְבַר

and the word of   מִירוּשָׁלָיִם

from Jerusalem   מִצִּיּוֹן

in God's holiness   שֶׁנָּתַן

who gave   לְעַמּוֹ

Torah, teaching   בִּקְדֻשָּׁתוֹ

With each tender act, parents can instill in their children an ability to love and nurture.

PRAYER VARIATIONS

As the Ark is opened, some congregations add the following words from the Torah (Numbers 10:35) before כִּי מִצִּיּוֹן.

וַיְהִי בִּנְסֹעַ הָאָרֹן וַיֹּאמֶר מֹשֶׁה:
קוּמָה יְיָ וְיָפֻצוּ אֹיְבֶיךָ, וְיָנֻסוּ מְשַׂנְאֶיךָ מִפָּנֶיךָ.

When the Ark was carried forward, Moses said:
Arise, Adonai; may Your enemies be scattered, may Your foes be driven to flight.

Other congregations do not mention war or the Jews' enemies, but add:

הָבוּ גֹדֶל לֵאלֹהֵינוּ וּתְנוּ כָבוֹד לַתּוֹרָה.

Let us declare God's greatness and give honor to the Torah.

No matter which words they add before כִּי מִצִּיּוֹן, all congregations are alike in praising God for giving us the Torah. Which version of the prayer is found in *your* synagogue's prayer book?

WHAT'S MISSING?

Circle the word that completes each sentence.

1. כִּי _____ תֵּצֵא תּוֹרָה
   from Zion

   מִצִּיוֹן   מִירוּשָׁלָיִם   לְעַמּוֹ

2. וּדְבַר יְיָ _____
   from Jerusalem

   תּוֹרָה   מִירוּשָׁלָיִם   מִצִּיוֹן

3. בָּרוּךְ שֶׁנָּתַן _____
   Torah

   יְיָ   יִשְׂרָאֵל   תּוֹרָה

4. לְעַמּוֹ _____ בִּקְדֻשָּׁתוֹ
   Israel

   יִשְׂרָאֵל   מִצִּיוֹן   וּדְבַר

OUT OF ORDER

Number the seven words from the first line
of כִּי מִצִּיוֹן in the correct order.

תֵּצֵא ◯   וּדְבַר ◯   תּוֹרָה ◯

מִצִּיוֹן ◯   מִירוּשָׁלָיִם ◯

יְיָ ◯   כִּי ◯

Number the six words from the second line
of כִּי מִצִּיוֹן in the correct order.

יִשְׂרָאֵל ◯   לְעַמּוֹ ◯

שֶׁנָּתַן ◯   בָּרוּךְ ◯

תּוֹרָה ◯   בִּקְדֻשָּׁתוֹ ◯

King David's Tower in the Old City
of Jerusalem.

3

Prayer Building Blocks

מִצִיוֹן "from Zion"

מִצִיוֹן is made up of two parts.

מִ is a prefix meaning "from."

צִיוֹן means "Zion."

מִצִיוֹן means _____.

Zion is another name for Jerusalem.

וּדְבַר "and the word of"

וּ is a prefix meaning _____.

דְבַר means "the word of."

Read the following sentences and circle all the words built on the root דבר ("speak," "word," or "thing").

1. וְהָיוּ הַדְּבָרִים הָאֵלֶּה, אֲשֶׁר אָנֹכִי מְצַוְּךָ הַיּוֹם, עַל לְבָבֶךָ.

2. בָּרוּךְ אַתָּה יְיָ, הָאֵל הַנֶּאֱמָן בְּכָל דְּבָרָיו.

3. וְעֵינֵינוּ תִרְאֶינָה מַלְכוּתֶךָ כַּדָּבָר הָאָמוּר בְּשִׁירֵי עֻזֶּךָ.

4. וְדָבָר אֶחָד מִדְּבָרֶיךָ אָחוֹר לֹא יָשׁוּב רֵיקָם.

5. הָאֵל הַנֶּאֱמָן, הָאוֹמֵר וְעוֹשֶׂה, הַמְדַבֵּר וּמְקַיֵּם.

💡 DID YOU KNOW?

In Hebrew, we refer to the Ten Commandments as עֲשֶׂרֶת הַדִּבְּרוֹת

Circle the root letters דבר in the second word: עֲשֶׂרֶת הַדִּבְּרוֹת

What does עֲשֶׂרֶת mean? _____

מִירוּשָׁלָיִם "from Jerusalem"

מִירוּשָׁלָיִם is made up of two parts.

מִ is a prefix meaning "from."

יְרוּשָׁלָיִם means "Jerusalem."

The prophet Isaiah first said the words כִּי מִצִּיּוֹן תֵּצֵא תוֹרָה, וּדְבַר־יְיָ מִירוּשָׁלָיִם

in his vision of a peaceful world in which "they shall beat their swords into plowshares" and "nation shall not lift up sword against nation" (Isaiah 2:3-4). Here, תוֹרָה means "teaching" or "instruction."

Read these sentences and underline the Hebrew word for Jerusalem in each one.

1. וּבְנֵה יְרוּשָׁלַיִם עִיר הַקֹּדֶשׁ בִּמְהֵרָה בְיָמֵינוּ.

2. אַב הָרַחֲמִים, הֵיטִיבָה בִרְצוֹנְךָ אֶת צִיּוֹן,
   תִּבְנֶה חוֹמוֹת יְרוּשָׁלָיִם.

3. תִּתְגַּדַּל וְתִתְקַדַּשׁ בְּתוֹךְ יְרוּשָׁלַיִם עִירְךָ.

4. בָּרוּךְ אַתָּה יְיָ, בּוֹנֶה בְרַחֲמָיו יְרוּשָׁלָיִם, אָמֵן.

5. שִׂמְחוּ אֶת יְרוּשָׁלַיִם וְגִילוּ בָה כָּל אֹהֲבֶיהָ.

Do you recognize the prayer in line 2?

Write its name here. _____

When do we say this prayer? _____

שֶׁנָּתַן "who gave"

שֶׁנָּתַן is made up of two parts.

שֶׁ is a prefix meaning "who."

נָתַן means "gave."

בָּרוּךְ שֶׁנָּתַן תּוֹרָה means "praised is the One who gave the Torah."

Who is the One who gave us the Torah? Write your answer in Hebrew. _____

לְעַמּוֹ "to God's people"

לְ is a prefix meaning "to."

עַמּוֹ means "God's people."

עַם means "people" or "nation."

וֹ at the end of a word means "his."

As God is neither male nor female, we translate לְעַמּוֹ as "to God's people."

בִּקְדֻשָּׁתוֹ "in God's holiness"

בְּ is a prefix meaning "in."

קְדֻשָּׁה means "holiness."

קְדֻשָּׁתוֹ means "God's holiness."

בִּקְדֻשָּׁתוֹ means _____.

What is the root of בִּקְדֻשָּׁתוֹ? ____ ____ ____

Circle the root letters קדש in each word below.

וַיְקַדֵּשׁ   הַקָּדוֹשׁ   מַקְדִּישִׁים   קָדְשְׁךָ

קָדוֹשׁ   וּקְדוֹשִׁים

What does קדש mean? _____

HOLDING THE TORAH

In many congregations, the person holding the Torah, after it is taken out of the Ark, recites each of the following lines, first alone, and then with the congregation. In other congregations, the lines are recited in unison.

שְׁמַע יִשְׂרָאֵל: יְיָ אֱלֹהֵינוּ, יְיָ אֶחָד.

Hear O Israel: Adonai is our God, Adonai is One.

אֶחָד אֱלֹהֵינוּ, גָּדוֹל אֲדוֹנֵינוּ, קָדוֹשׁ שְׁמוֹ.

Our God is One and is great; God's name is holy.

A third line is added. In some congregations, the person holding the Torah turns to face the Ark and bows when this line is recited.

גַּדְּלוּ לַיְיָ אִתִּי וּנְרוֹמְמָה שְׁמוֹ יַחְדָּו.

Acclaim Adonai with me, and together let us exalt God's name.

When you become a Bar or Bat Mitzvah you will have the honor of holding the most sacred possession of the Jewish people.

FLUENT READING

Each line below contains a word you know. Practice reading the lines.

1. בָּרוּךְ אַתָּה, יְיָ, הָאֵל הַנֶּאֱמָן בְּכָל דְּבָרָיו.

2. אוֹר חָדָשׁ עַל צִיּוֹן תָּאִיר וְנִזְכֶּה כֻלָּנוּ מְהֵרָה לְאוֹרוֹ.

3. וּבְדִבְרֵי קָדְשְׁךָ כָּתוּב לֵאמֹר: יִמְלֹךְ יְיָ לְעוֹלָם אֱלֹהַיִךְ צִיּוֹן לְדֹר וָדֹר הַלְלוּיָהּ.

4. אִם אֶשְׁכָּחֵךְ יְרוּשָׁלָיִם תִּשְׁכַּח יְמִינִי.

5. גָּדוֹל יְיָ וּמְהֻלָּל מְאֹד וְלִגְדֻלָּתוֹ אֵין חֵקֶר.

6. כִּי בָנוּ בָחַרְתָּ וְאוֹתָנוּ קִדַּשְׁתָּ.

7. רְצֵה יְיָ אֱלֹהֵינוּ בְּעַמְּךָ יִשְׂרָאֵל וּבִתְפִלָּתָם.

8. הָאֵל הַגָּדוֹל הַגִּבּוֹר וְהַנּוֹרָא, אֵל עֶלְיוֹן.

9. בָּרוּךְ אַתָּה, יְיָ, הַבּוֹחֵר בַּתּוֹרָה, וּבְמֹשֶׁה עַבְדּוֹ, וּבְיִשְׂרָאֵל עַמּוֹ, וּבִנְבִיאֵי הָאֱמֶת וָצֶדֶק.

10. לִהְיוֹת עַם חָפְשִׁי בְּאַרְצֵנוּ, אֶרֶץ צִיּוֹן וִירוּשָׁלָיִם.

Copyright © 2004 by Behrman House, Inc; Springfield, NJ; www.behrmanhouse.com; Author: Terry Kaye; Contributing Authors: Claudia Grossman and Lori Justice; Photographs: Richard Lobell (2), Gila Gevirtz (3), Ginny Twersky (7). ISBN 0-87441-764-3 (Ki Mitziyon); Manufactured in the United States of America. Artist: Ilene Winn-Lederer